think
good
thoughts
about a
pussycat

think
good
thoughts
about a
pussycat

george booth

 A FLARE BOOK / PUBLISHED BY AVON BOOKS

AVON BOOKS
A division of
The Hearst Corporation
959 Eighth Avenue
New York, New York 10019

To William and Norene,
Gaylord and James

ABOUT GEORGE

THE MATERNAL HEART leaped with joy, though common sense warned, "Wait, wait! It may not last." Three-and-one half-year-old George had just shown me his first cartoon—an old Model T stuck in the mud. To him it was funny. To me, portentous. Was this what my dream of becoming a cartoonist had accomplished?

As he pushed pencil after pencil through ream after ream of paper, passing through the grades, through the growing pains and through high school, my heart kept leaping, but the warning kept restraining me, saying, "Wait and see. Tomorrow he may decide to become a herpetologist."

His aim was art school, but the Marines sent him to Parris Island, then to the Pacific. After VJ Day, the *Leatherneck*, tired of being bombarded with his submissions, sent for him. He arrived in D.C. with a wet wash and a hot iron. There he learned some of the finer points of cartooning such as refraining from drawing hungry Marines eating out of Navy garbage cans.

Then he served a hitch at the Chicago Academy of Fine Arts, another with the Marines and *Leatherneck*, thence to New York where he rolled with *Tide* magazine, worked for Bill Communications, then free lance, and finally happily got a foot caught in the door at *New Yorker*.

You think I'm proud? Yes, I am proud I had the privilege of watching him, of drawing and having fun with him all along the way. Stay in there, George. I think you are going to make it.

*"I want you to start thinking good thoughts about someone <u>new</u> at our house.
I want you to start thinking good thoughts about a pussy cat."*

"And do you, Elizabeth, take this man, John, to have and to hold, to love and to cherish, until the going gets hairy?"

"*Have you and your bear ever had a loan with us before?*"

"*We'll have to keep your car another day. There's a devilled egg in the carburetor.*"

BOOTH

"Would it be technically feasible, Hussan, to make pots that would disintegrate after a few years?"

"The artist was unknown when Harold discovered him and he's still unknown, except, of course, that he and Harold are acquainted now."

KEEPING WARM

On sunny cold days, carry clothes in suitcase and quickly pinch on Kitchen-foil suit.

Turkey pan (foil $1.29) will work best for quick Pinch-on cap.

Heated BB boots.

← CORK

Sew canvas boots. Slip on over shoes.

Fill with hot BBs. BBs heat fast in an iron skillet.

Heated tire irons wrapped in towels can be carried under one's topcoat.

Hot-water tie. Warm all day at the office.

Face catnip comforter.

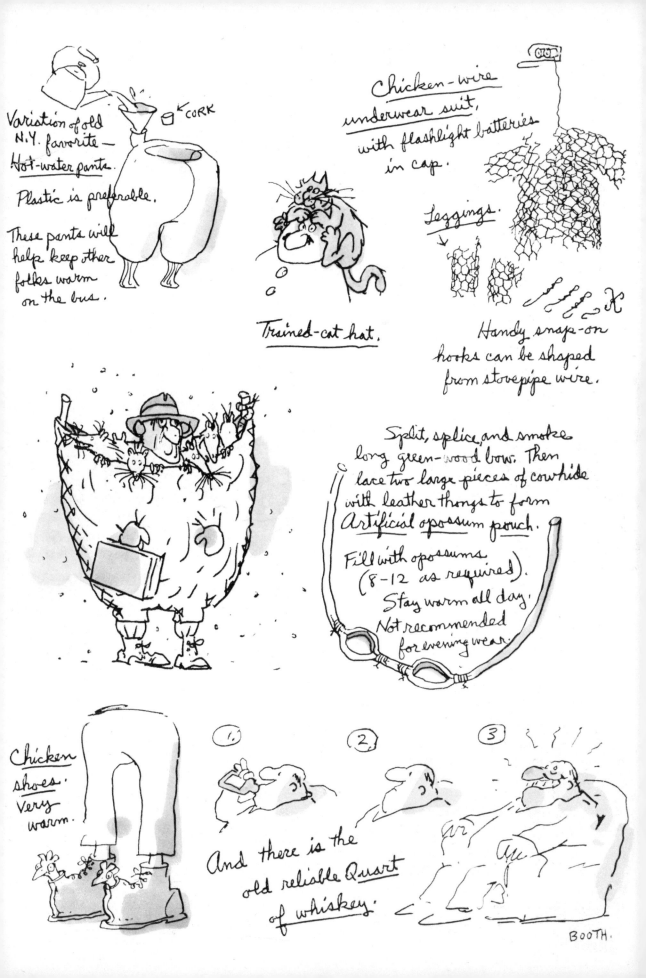

Variation of old N.Y. favorite—
~~Hot-water pants.~~

Plastic is preferable.

These pants will help keep other folks warm on the bus.

CORK

Trained-cat hat.

Chicken-wire underwear suit, with flashlight batteries in cap.

Leggings.

Handy snap-on hooks can be shaped from stovepipe wire.

Split, splice, and smoke long green-wood bow. Then lace two large pieces of cowhide with leather thongs to form Artificial opossum pouch.

Fill with opossums (8–12 as required).
Stay warm all day.
Not recommended for evening wear.

Chicken shoes. Very warm.

① ② ③

And there is the old reliable Quart of whiskey.

BOOTH.

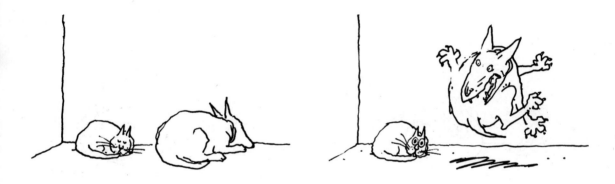

BOOTH

"De Witt and the refrigerator blew out about the same time."

"*The lady has a point! After drinking all day long, how <u>can</u> a woman go home to her children and say, 'Children, get your jammies on'?*"

"Oh, my father was the keeper of the Eddystone Light.
 He slept with a mer-i-maid one fine night.
From this union there came threeeee:
 A porpoise, a porgy, and the other was meeeee.
Yo-ho-hooooo, the wind blows freeeeee . . ."

"Was it a 'ittle putty tat?
'es it was. It was a putty!
Tum tum tum!
Tum on, pwetty putty,
tum det on Mommy's wap."

"*Launch the hoary desperados, fugitive debtors and bankrupt peasants in that order . . . before evening repast!*"

BOOTH

"Aphids on the heliotrope!"

BOOTH

"Do you know what I'm going to do? I'm going to pull my hat down over one eye and frizzle my hair."

"*Now, last time, near the end of Ravel's 'Bolero,' I heard a scream.*"

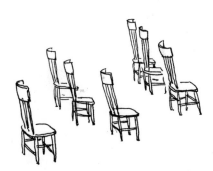

BOOTH

"Is it all right to serve him the
Executive Special?"

"*How are the vital signs this morning, Seth?*"

"I was just eighteen when dashing Jamie Benton looked at me in <u>bold</u> admiration. There was a tight feeling about my heart, and for a moment I thought I would swoon. In the days that followed, I was courted with wine and roses and Shakespeare. My soul awoke with a gasp, and in the very instant of awakening went out to him forever. Today, however, I feel privileged to get so much as a grunt out of the old curmudgeon."

"*What the hell do you mean you don't sell tickets to Larchmont?*"

"Say something nice to me, Luke. Not anything common. Something that
will rekindle smoldering passions, stoke the memory of half-forgotten
follies, and make the fountains of my spirit flow again."

"It seems some days like I make a little progress, then other days
it seems like I'm not getting anywhere at all."

BOOTH

"Your bill comes to forty-eight dollars more than we estimated, because
that little black thing with a lot of wires going into it needed fixing."

BOOTH

"If you withdraw or deposit your damn five dollars one more time this year, Mrs. Babcock, I'm going to shoot you!"

"Harry, I wish you'd stop singing 'The Impossible Dream' and
help me feed the pussies once in a while."

BOOTH

BOOTH

"Guess what, everybody. Mrs. Fancher is going to visit her daughter in Florida, and her Cissus rhombifolia is coming to stay with us for a few weeks."

"You give me my 'Cosmopolitan' or I'll whop you!"

"*Here, Shih Tzu Dong! Here, Shih Tzu Dong! Din-din!*"

"One of the choir boys tells me Ralph Nader is hiding in the lilies."

*"Ferguson, do you have days when you don't
feel a cut above the rest?"*

"Burgess has enjoyed his evening paper as long as I've known him. It's only recently he's developed that graveyard laugh."

BOOTH

"*Having concluded, Your Highness, an exhaustive study of this nation's political, social, and economic history, and after examining, Sire, the unfortunate events leading to the present deplorable state of the realm, the consensus of the Council is that Your Majesty's only course, for the public good, must be to take the next step.*"

"*Honeywell knows what makes people tick.*"

"*The air I breathe is filthy, my food is poisoned, my automobile is a gas-guzzling behemoth, my school taxes have doubled, the Internal Revenue Service plans to take the fillings out of my teeth, my wife is fifty-three and pregnant, my dog bit a lawyer's kid, my son steals, my mother-in-law is a Communist, my daughter ran off with a fink, and now you tell me that if I don't back up and let you have the right-of-way I'll be in trouble.*"

"Hippety-hop, hippety-hop, hippety-hop."

"*Other folks have to pay taxes, too, Mr. Herndon, so would you please spare us the dramatics!*"

"I know what we need, Hartford, honey . . . we need a change of pace . . .
that's what we need . . . we need a change of pace . . .
it just came to me . . . we need a change of pace . . .
what do you think about that . . . I mean about a change of pace . . .
don't you think we need a change of pace?"

"You dawdle, daydream. You make lists of things to do but can't get started. You seem to be restricted from doing what you know you should be doing. These problems will dissolve when you read Chapter Ten of my new book, at eight dollars and ninety-five cents."

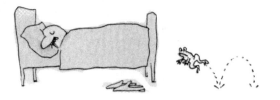

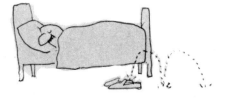

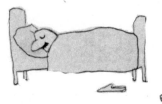

BOOTH

*"We'll have your car ready to go in just a few minutes, Mr. Henderson . . .
just as soon as Tony finds your radiator hose."*

"Management has asked us all to tighten our belts a bit."

"*Artificial coloring, artificial flavoring, artificial glop, artificial slop, artificial this, artificial that . . .*"

"Kaboom!"

"*I want it clearly understood that I am casting no aspersions on my wife's cooking. Heh heh, heh heh, heh heh, heh heh, heh heh heh, heh heh, heh heh, heh heh, heh heh heh, heh heh, heh heh, heh heh heh, heh heh. . . .*"

BOOTH

BOOTH

"The time of assertion and counter-assertion is upon us."

"*Gee, Al, that's the first time I ever heard 'Tennessee Birdwalk' played on the trombone.*"

"I'll run through it again. First, the exhilaration of a work completed, followed by the excitement of approaching pub date. Reviews pouring in from everywhere while the bidding for the paperback rights soars to insane figures. An appearance on Merv Griffin or Dick Cavett, sandwiched in between like Engelbert Humperdinck and Juliet Prowse. Finally, a flood of letters from people to whom your name, yesterday unknown, now has the shimmer of national renown. Hit those keys!"

"Say! The Purple Onion wants impersonators."

"A _free_ Thunderbird key chain from the veterans, 'Time' sent another little bitty pencil, Pampero Mission sent greeting cards and enclosed a snapshot of a sick Indian, and 'Reader's Digest' says you may already be a winner."

"*Attention, Mr. Bargain Hunter: One pair Arctic snowshoes, one genuine coon-skin cap (medium), and one complete set of the World's Most Honored Music by the Longines Symphonette. Will sell or swap for samurai sword, Luftwaffe staff uniform, or other World War II memorabilia.*"

"*The men feel there is an evil spirit in your clutch housing. We've called a priest.*"

"Some DAAAAAY my prince will come . . ."

"*You filled an old tire with marigolds. I never said a word. You planted petunias in a potbellied stove. I kept my mouth shut. You put geraniums in the birdbath. I didn't say anything. This morning, you filled that damned old white enamel washing machine with morning glories, and <u>now</u>, by God, I'm going to say something.*"

"Did you yawp, sir?"

"*You may as well have a seat, Buster. The boys have had an eighteen-car collision on the upper ramps.*"

*"Aside from your three-dollar lottery
ticket, have you any collateral, Mr. Shelton?"*

"We are, of course, unable to reprint menus to accurately reflect our constantly changing food costs. In strict accordance with price regulations, a small charge will be added to the menu items to cover our actual increased purchasing price. We ask that you bear with us during this difficult period."

"*You want my opinion. My opinion is that when push comes to shove, it will be more bad news for the consumer.*"

BOOTH

"Oh, Lester! Not my macramé!"

*"From this day forward, we will do our very best to do unto
Pussy as we would have Pussy do unto us."*

"I think,"

"therefore I am."

"I think."

BOOTH

"*Attention, everyone! Here comes Poppa, and we're going to drive dull care away! It's quips and cranks and wanton wiles, nods and becks and wreathed smiles.*"

"*Shame on you, Jamie! Mr. Huntington will be here in a few minutes
and he'll say, 'Henry, is my car ready?' And what
am I going to say? . . . Am I going to say,
'Mr. Huntington . . . Jamie made a boo-boo'?*"

"*Harold, would you say you are left of center, right of center, center, left of left, right of left, left of right, or right of right, or what?*"

BOOTH

"If Iggie Goldfarb wants to play 'Death of a Salesman' every morning of the year for thirty years, I say *let* Iggie Goldfarb play 'Death of a Salesman' every morning of the year for thirty years."

"*We were minding our own business when the paddy wagon pulled up and took the good girls with the bad girls.*"

*"If you ask me, this thing is going
to get a whole lot worse before it gets better."*

"Woonk doesn't know any words, but he's the best there is
when it comes to the grunt, the snort, and the howl."

"*Approximately one-third of our income goes for defense.*"

"*I ran into Mrs. Spencer today. She's giving
serious consideration to origami.*"

"Would you see to old Peterson? He's in the philodendron again."

"*Three years in a row, Hoot's lespedeza went moldy. His chickens got sick and quit laying. He tried mixing his own anti-freeze and busted both tractor blocks. Then Coolidge, his favorite mule, slipped in the barn lot and died. It just seemed like one bad omen after another. So finally Hoot says, 'It's either shoot the cattle or run for Congress.' Well, Hoot ain't one to shoot animals, but you can bet your bottom dollar he'll tell those other congressmen what's what up there in Washington.*"

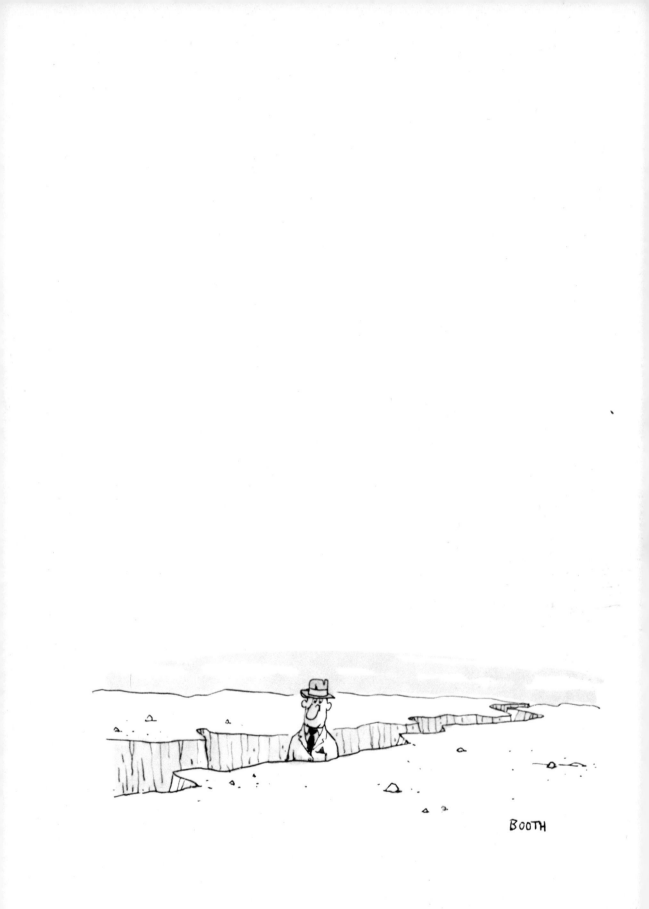

"Since the new flexible working hours began, Seymour,
we haven't been able to locate yours."

"*The seventies are going to be perkier than the sixties were.*"

BOOTH

"*It's my observation that more and more consumers are looking after their own interests these days.*"

"A rose is a . . . sort of like I mean a . . . you know . . .
rose . . . is . . . like . . . you know . . . a rose . . . right?"

BOOTH

"*All the pieces in this room are for sale except the chifforobe. The chifforobe is <u>not</u> for sale.*"

*"The pivotal issue, then, is not whether
you respond to my needs by cash or by
check but for how much."*

BOOTH

*"I call this spot Templeton's End, because this is where I dumped
Old Templeton into the bog—Newport wheelchair and all."*

"How long have you been gone now, Templeton?"

"Whistle, you dumb bastard!"

"When Jamie ate the stamps, I told him Mr. Postman would be very angry. And you *are* very angry,
aren't you, Mr. Postman?"

" 'It is not what a man gets but what a man is that he should think of. He should think first of his character, and then of his condition, for if he have the former, he need have no fear about the latter. Character will draw condition after it. Circumstances obey principles.'—Henry Ward Beecher."

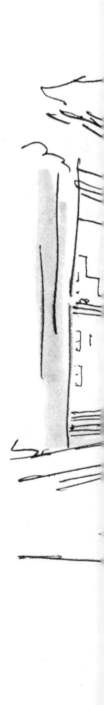

"*Smmneff smmneff Bot nak il ttidi wonn gllnett oy oy pwwrin
walll gges nup uuop smmneff bot oyoy reaa sop!*"

BOOTH

"Claypoole has his __up__ days and he has his __down__ days. Today, he seems to be tipping over."

"You get no interest on your account, Mrs. Dunwoodie, because your day
of deposit and your day of withdrawal were the same damn day."

"Give me a W. Give me an O. Give me an R. Give me a K. I want an E. I want a T. Give me an H and an I and a C."

"*My amaryllis is in bloom, my bougainvillea is in bloom, my geranium tree is in bloom, and, though I'm not mentioning any more names, there's someone else around here who needs to bloom a little, too.*"

"I'd just like to know what in hell is happening, that's all! I'd like to know what in hell is happening! Do _you_ know what in hell is happening?"

*"Templeton should be here shortly with a first-hand report
on the Forty-second Street pornography problem."*

BOOTH

"How about supper in the tub tonight, Hon?"

"On my way home today on the bus, a lone grape rolled down the aisle and came to rest near my foot. It was pale green and looked to be of the seedless variety."

BOOTH